ZRjC
3118

# Favorite Fairies

Illustrated by The Disney Storybook Artists

This library edition published in 2014 by Walter Foster Jr.,
an imprint of Quarto Publishing Group USA Inc.
6 Orchard Road, Suite 100
Lake Forest, CA 92630

Distributed in the United States and Canada by
Lerner Publisher Services
241 First Avenue North
Minneapolis, MN 55401 U.S.A.
www.lernerbooks.com

First Library Edition

Library of Congress Cataloging-in-Publication Data

Learn to draw Disney favorite fairies / illustrated by the Disney Storybook Artists. -- Library edition.
    pages cm
ISBN 978-1-93958-113-6
1.  Fairies in art--Juvenile literature. 2.  Disney characters in art--Juvenile literature. 3.  Drawing--
Technique--Juvenile literature.  I. Disney Storybook Artists, illustrator.
  NC825.F22L43 2014
  741.5'1--dc23
                                                                                    2013025000


9 8 7 6 5 4 3

# Table of Contents

Every fairy starts out as a baby's first laugh, and this story is about one very special laugh. It traveled all the way from wintry London to the magical land of Pixie Hollow. There, the laugh touched down in the Pixie Dust Tree and became a fairy! All around the new fairy, toadstools sprung up like pedestals. Fairies came forward and placed different objects on the toadstools—a drop of water, a flower, a tiny egg, and more—to help the new arrival find her talent.

The new fairy cautiously approached each object. At first, nothing happened, but when she passed by a small hammer, it began to glow brightly. The fairy Queen, Queen Clarion, declared that the new fairy was a tinker—

and a very powerful one! Her name was Tinker Bell.

Tinker Bell's first day was a busy one. First she met Clank and Bobble, two other tinkers, and Fairy Mary, the fairy in charge of the workshop in Tinkers' Nook. Later, she helped deliver tools to other fairies. While Tinker Bell was out making deliveries with her new friends, she met Fawn, Rosetta, Iridessa, and Silvermist. They were fairies, too, and Tink liked them immediately. On the way back to Tinkers' Nook, Tink met Vidia, a fast-flying fairy.

Tinker Bell grew in her talents as a tinker, and she loves living in Pixie Hollow. When the fairies aren't changing the seasons or performing their given tasks, they love to participate in the Pixie Hollow Games. Garden fairies Chloe and Rosetta team up against undefeated storm fairies Glimmer and Rumble for a particularly exciting round of the games.

On one of her many adventures, Tinker Bell wanders into the mysterious Winter Woods and meets Periwinkle, a frost fairy who loves to slide down frozen waterfalls! She and Tinker Bell become fast friends on their adventure together.

# Tools & Materials

The art fairies of Pixie Hollow use tiny, delicate twig-and-feather paintbrushes to paint the spots on ladybugs. But all you'll need for this book are normal, human-sized supplies. To begin, sketch your fairy with a regular pencil. You'll want to have a pencil sharpener and an eraser on hand as well. When you've drawn your fairies just the way you want them, you can bring them to life with a little color! Use crayons, felt-tip markers, colored pencils, or even paints to color in your fairies.

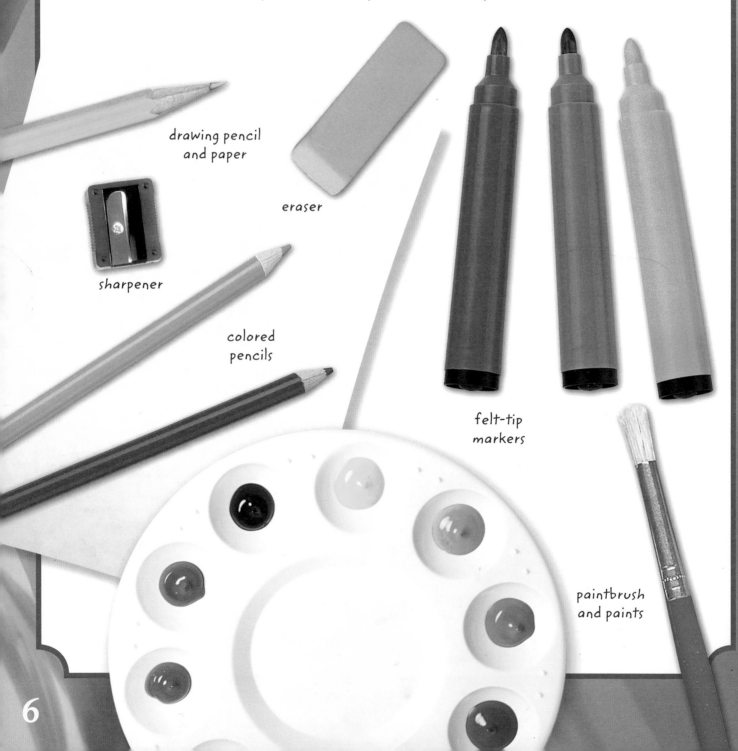

drawing pencil and paper

eraser

sharpener

colored pencils

felt-tip markers

paintbrush and paints

# How to Use This Book

You don't need the skills of an art fairy to follow these simple steps!

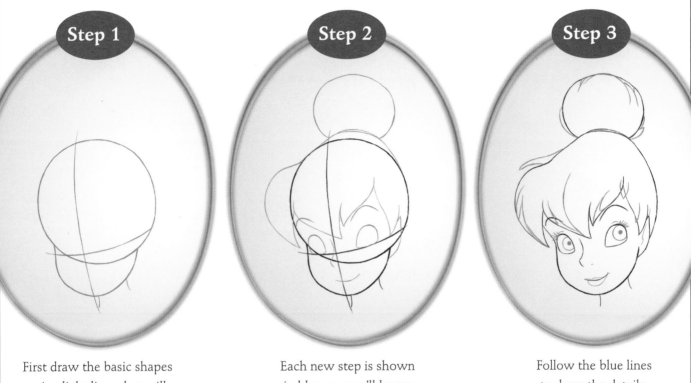

**Step 1**

First draw the basic shapes using light lines that will be easy to erase.

**Step 2**

Each new step is shown in blue, so you'll know what to add next.

**Step 3**

Follow the blue lines to draw the details.

**Step 4**

Now darken the lines you want to keep, and erase the rest.

**Step 5**

Use fairy magic (or crayons or markers) to add color to your drawing!

# Tinker Bell

This spirited tinker fairy arrives in Pixie Hollow by way of a baby's laugh in London. Her specialty is inventing things using objects from the mainland that wash up on the shores of Never Land. Tink has a big imagination—and an even bigger heart!

**Step 1**

**Step 2**

**Step 3**

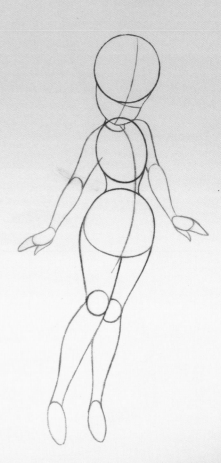

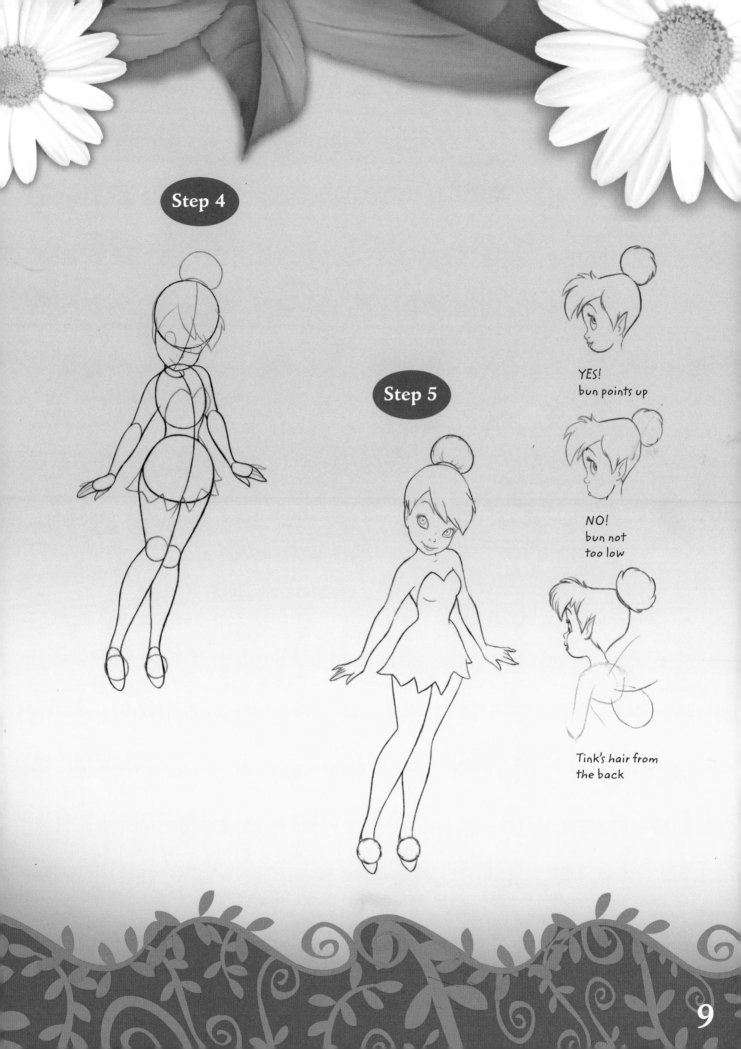

Step 4

Step 5

YES!
bun points up

NO!
bun not
too low

Tink's hair from
the back

9

**Step 6**

**Step 7**

YES!
bottom of skirt
pointy like leaves

NO!
bottom of skirt not
shaped like *flower*
petals

YES!
eye shape
rounded

NO!
not almond
shaped

# Tinker Bell Action

Tinker Bell has a feisty personality that allows her to be brave and perseverant, even when she gets frustrated because she can't fix something. She wears a green leaf dress that she designed herself!

**Step 1**

**Step 2**

**Step 3**

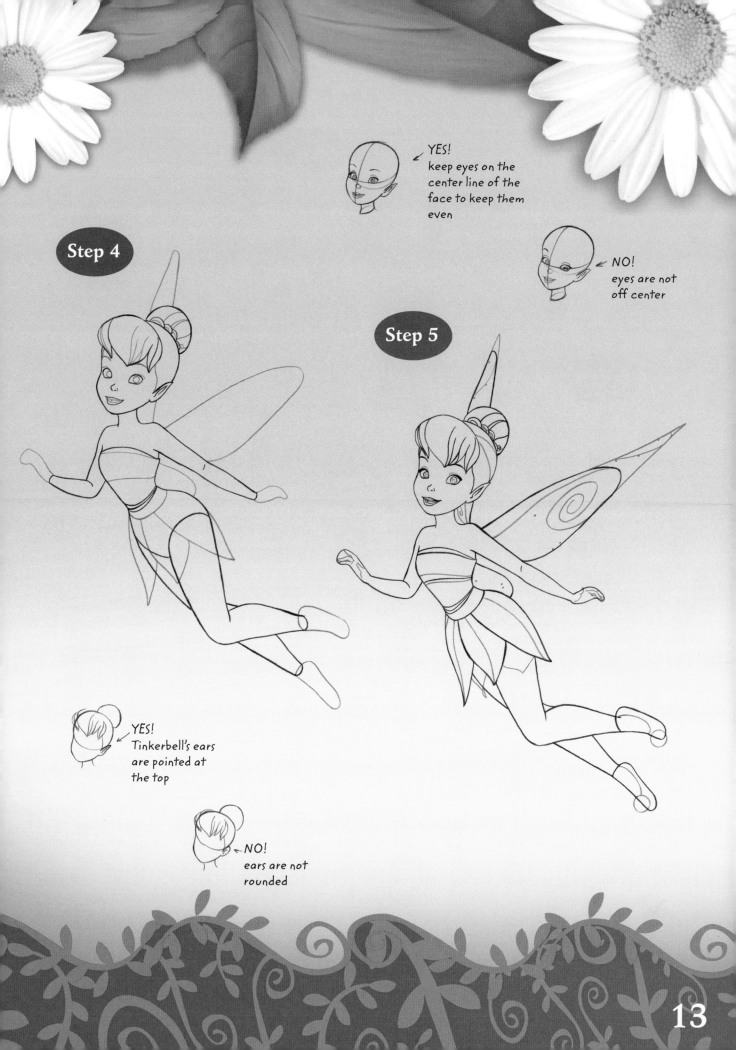

YES!
keep eyes on the
center line of the
face to keep them
even

NO!
eyes are not
off center

**Step 4**

**Step 5**

YES!
Tinkerbell's ears
are pointed at
the top

NO!
ears are not
rounded

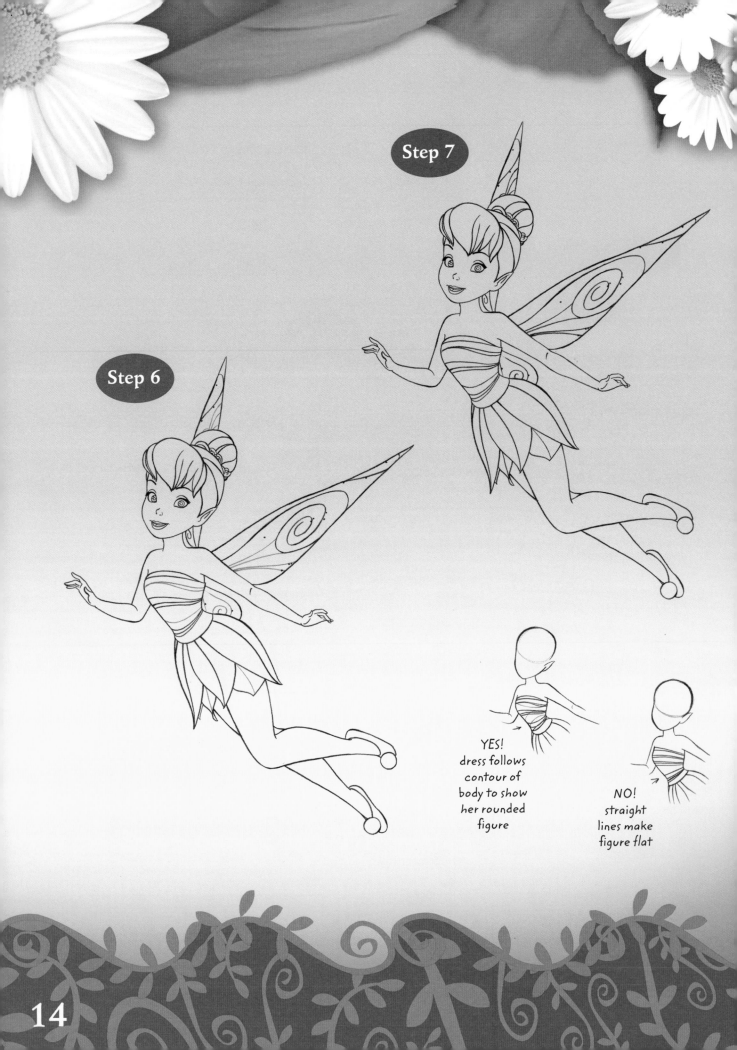

Step 7

Step 6

YES!
dress follows
contour of
body to show
her rounded
figure

NO!
straight
lines make
figure flat

# Periwinkle

Periwinkle lives in the Winter Woods, where she makes frost swirls and slides down frozen waterfalls for fun! She wears a dress that shimmers like ice and sports a cute, frosty up-do to match.

Step 1

Step 2

Step 3

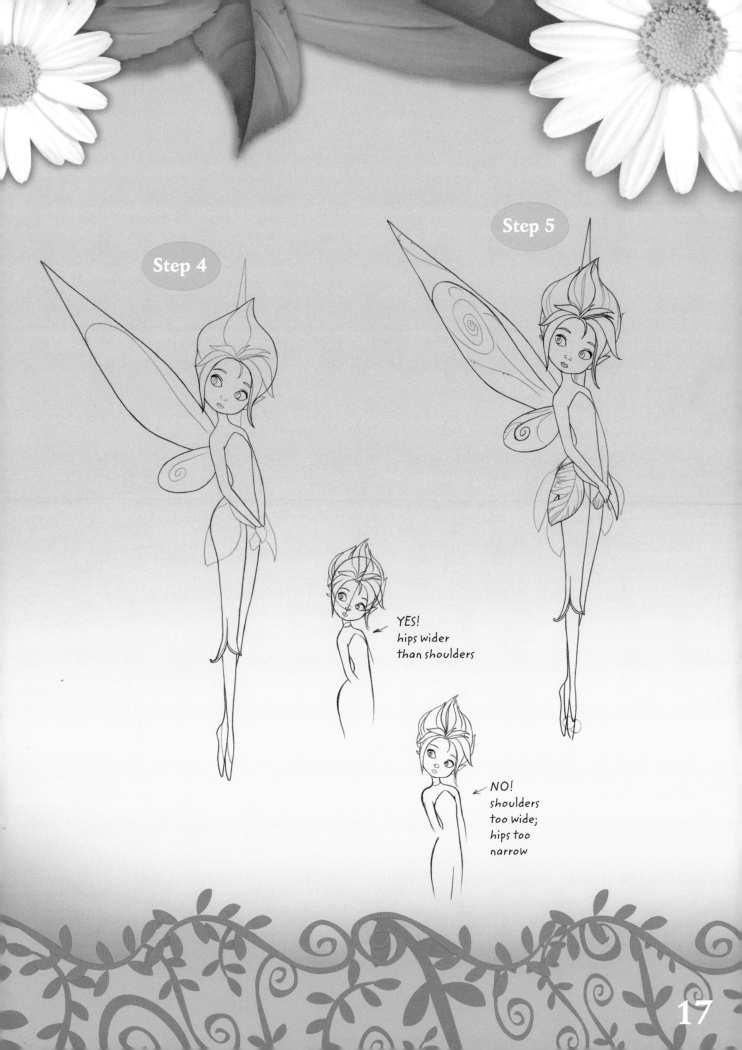

Step 4

Step 5

YES!
hips wider
than shoulders

NO!
shoulders
too wide;
hips too
narrow

Step 6

Step 7

YES!
keep eyes large
and open wide

NO!
eyes are
too small

# Fairy Mary

Fairy Mary is the stern, hardworking leader of the tinker fairies. She keeps everything running smoothly in Tinkers' Nook and takes great pride in her talent. She and Tink don't always see eye to eye, but they have great respect for each other.

Step 1

Step 2

Step 3

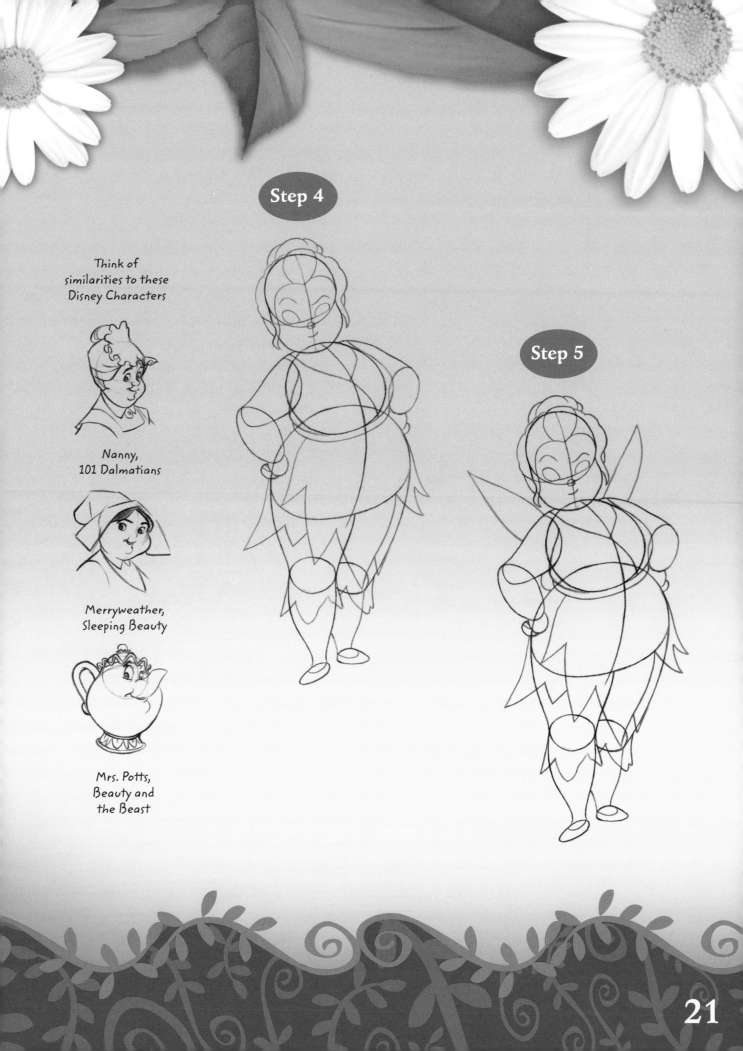

**Step 4**

**Step 5**

Think of similarities to these Disney Characters

Nanny,
101 Dalmatians

Merryweather,
Sleeping Beauty

Mrs. Potts,
Beauty and
the Beast

Step 6

Step 7

round shapes
create body
structure

22

sometimes carries an abacus— a tool for counting

# Silvermist

Friendly and eager to please, the water fairy Silvermist has occasionally been described as "gushy." She's got a good heart, even if she does seem to change her mind every ten minutes!

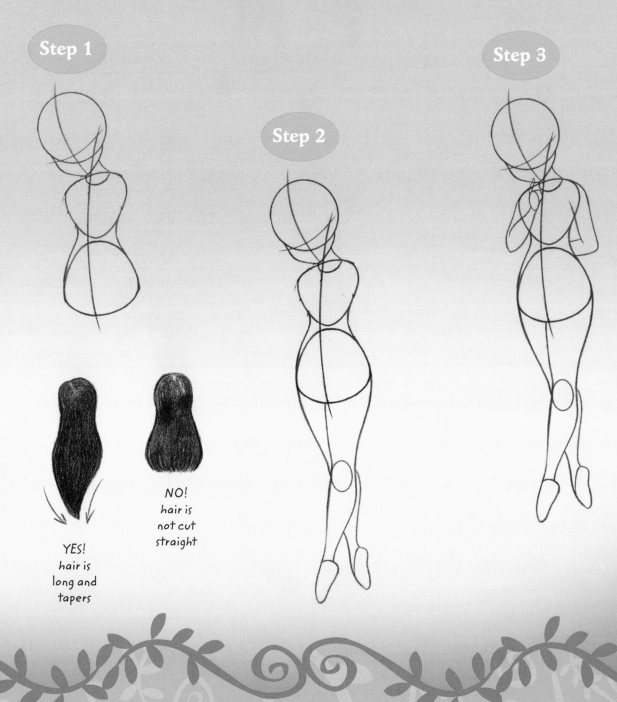

**Step 1**

**Step 2**

**Step 3**

YES!
hair is
long and
tapers

NO!
hair is
not cut
straight

**Step 4**

**Step 5**

strand of hair
falls in front of
one shoulder

Step 6

Step 7

Silvermist's dress is
made from lily petals

YES!
eyes set
at angle

NO!
eyes not
set on
straight
line

# Rosetta

Rosetta, a garden fairy, has a quick wit and a ton of charm.
Beautiful and sensible, Rosetta sees right to the heart of every problem.
Rosetta teams up with Chloe in the Pixie Hollow Games.

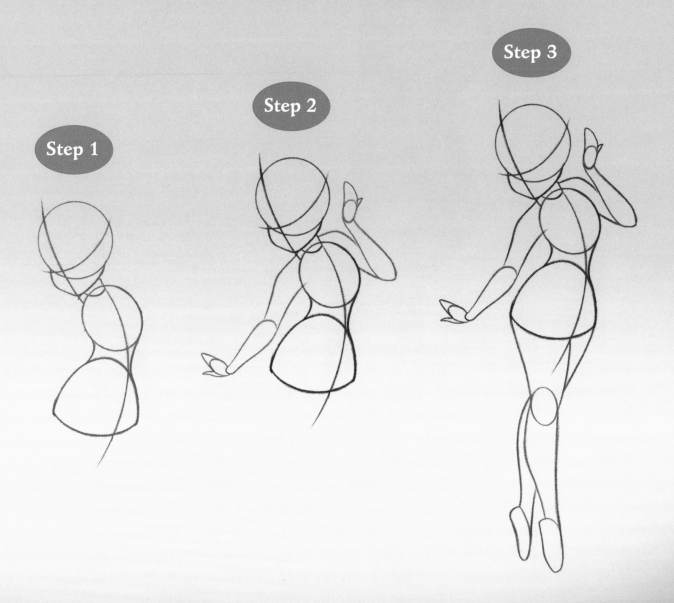

Step 1

Step 2

Step 3

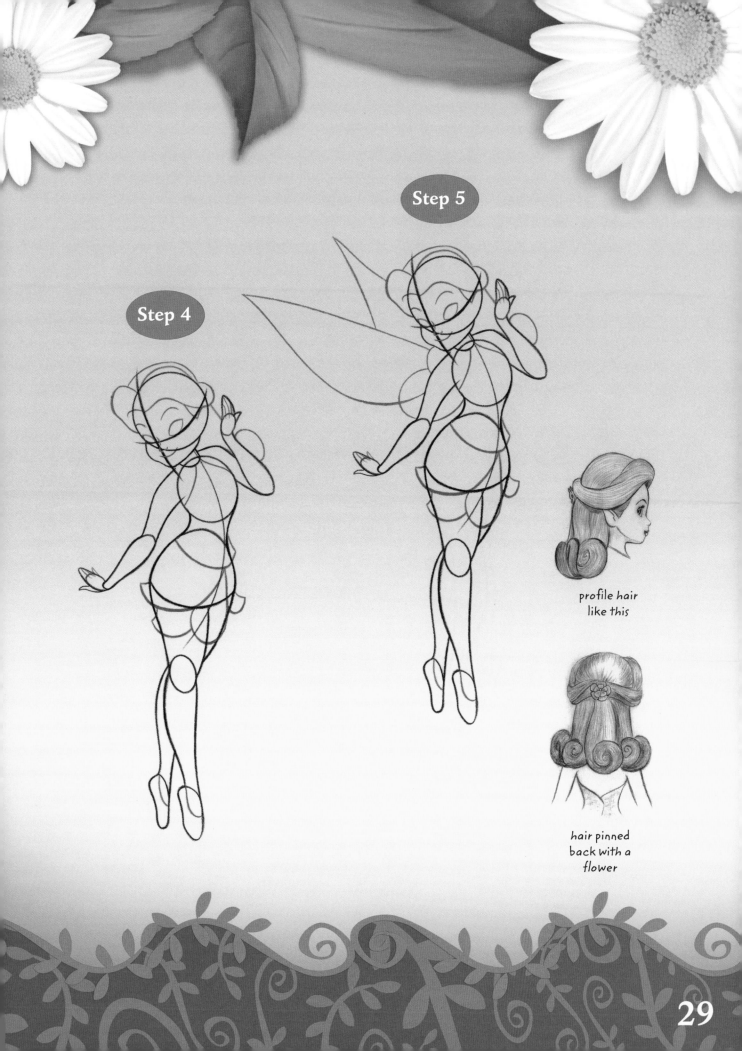

Step 4

Step 5

profile hair
like this

hair pinned
back with a
flower

Step 6

Step 7

Rosetta's dress
is made from
rose petals

YES!

NO!

# Iridessa

Iridessa is a thoughtful fairy who likes to do everything exactly right, especially when it comes to her job. No other light fairy catches the last rays of sunlight with quite the same precision as Iridessa.

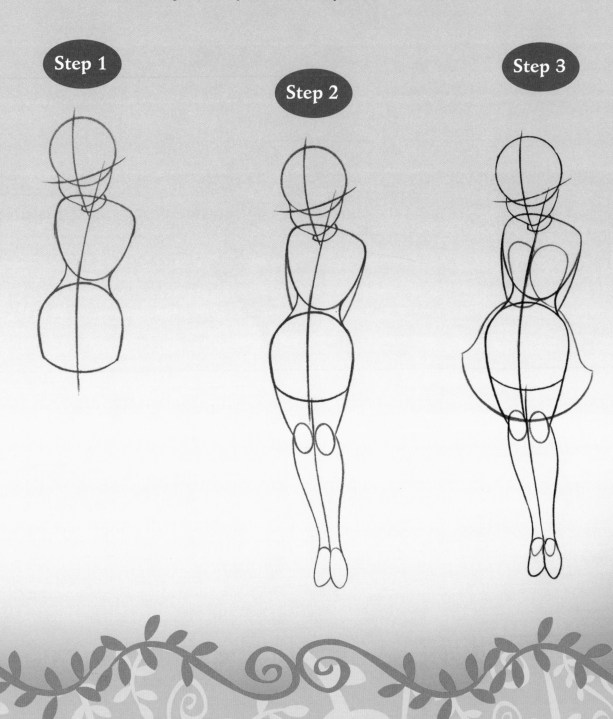

Step 4

Step 5

YES!
hair in
sections

YES!
slender chin,
full lips

NO!
cheeks not
too full

NO!
hair not
smooth

**Step 6**

**Step 7**

*Iridessa's top is made from a flower petal held in place by a sunflower seed*

34

skirt made
from sunflower
petals

35

# Fawn

Fawn is the greatest prankster Pixie Hollow has ever known, but she's also the biggest softie. She loves the animals she cares for, and they love her.

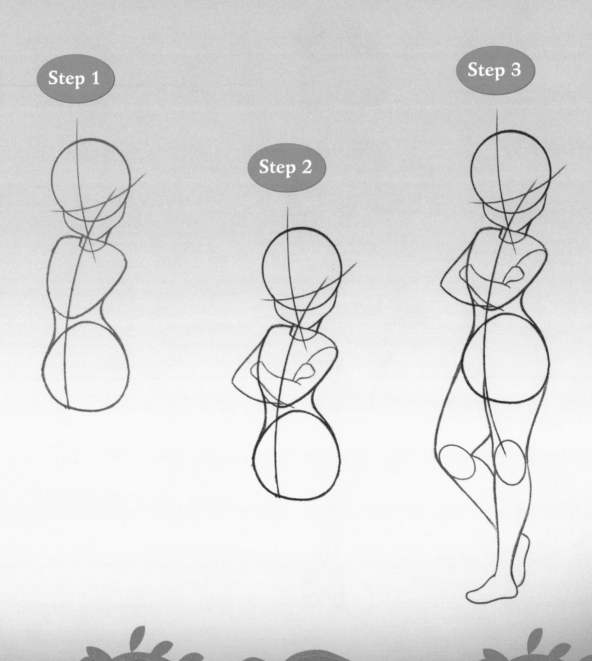

Step 1

Step 2

Step 3

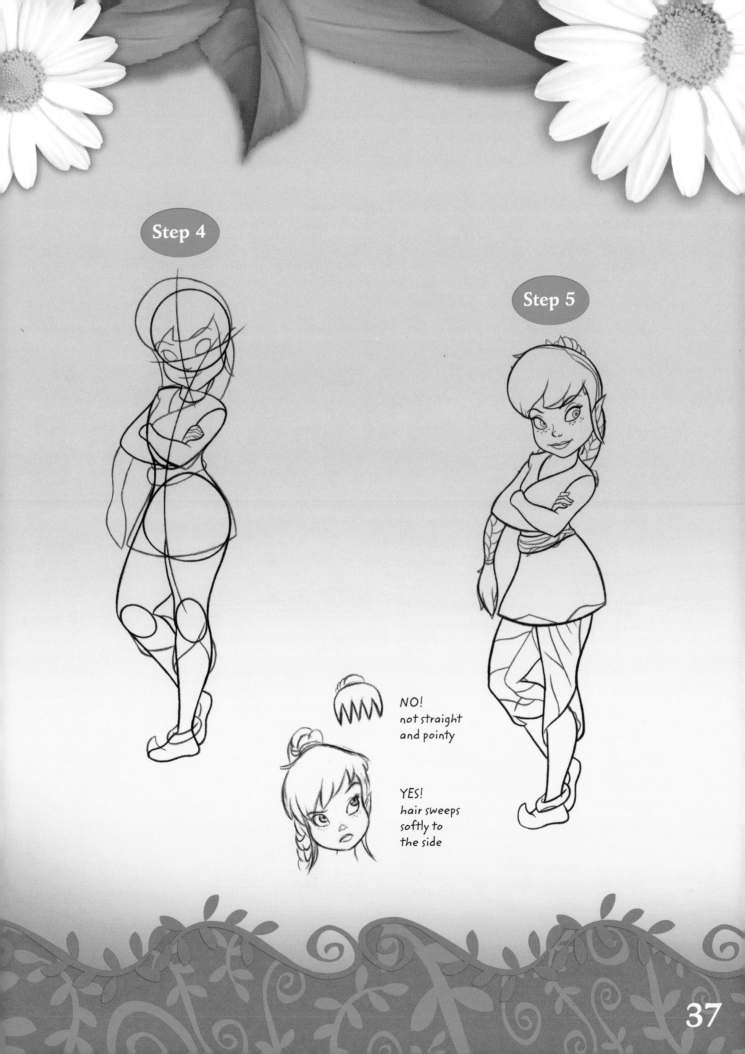

**Step 4**

**Step 5**

NO!
not straight
and pointy

YES!
hair sweeps
softly to
the side

**Step 6**

**Step 7**

cute, small,
upturned nose

wings attach in
middle of back

top wings
longer and
taper to a
point

bottom wings
smaller and
rounded

# Vidia

Spiteful Vidia loves being known for her talent and resents any competition—especially from Tinker Bell. But Vidia's schemes against Tink backfire, and the fast-flying fairy is left with the thankless job of rounding up the Sprinting Thistles.

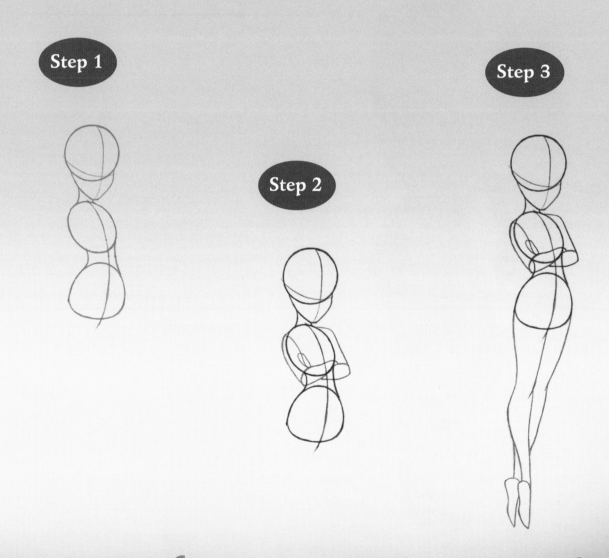

Step 1

Step 2

Step 3

NO!
eyelashes and
eyebrow not soft
and round

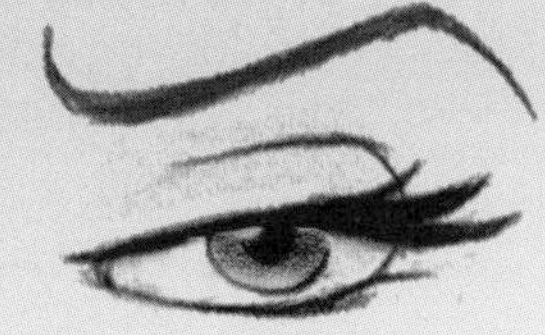

YES!
long, angled
eyebrow and
narrow eyes

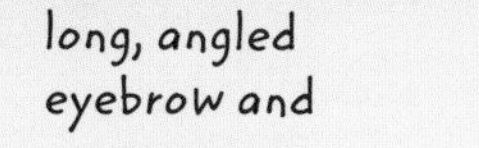

three thick
eyelashes like
heavy mascara
was applied

Step 4

Step 5

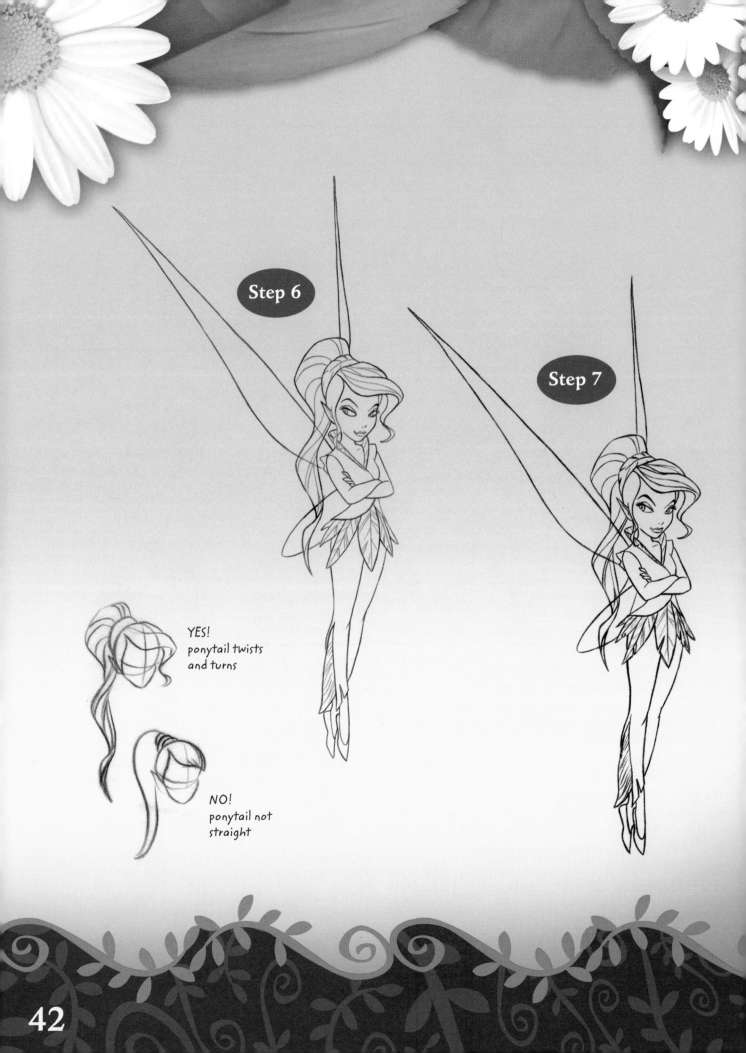

Step 6

Step 7

YES!
ponytail twists
and turns

NO!
ponytail not
straight

42

# Queen Clarion

Queen Clarion is the wise ruler of the fairies. Her magic is so powerful that she sometimes travels in a mist of pure pixie dust.

Step 1

Step 2

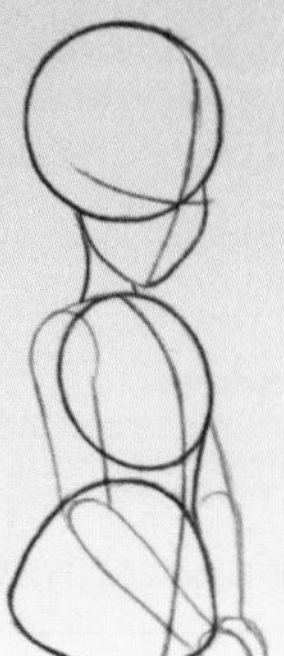

Step 3

**Step 5**

**Step 4**

Queen Clarion wears three different crowns for separate occasions

everyday crown

arrival crown

spring crown

YES!
eyes are
almond
shaped

NO!
not too
round

Step 7

Step 6

Queen Clarion's
wings are like a
butterfly's

# Terence

Terence is a dust-keeper fairy and Tinker Bell's best friend. He knows how important each and every fairy talent is and takes great pride in the work he does for the fairies of Pixie Hollow.

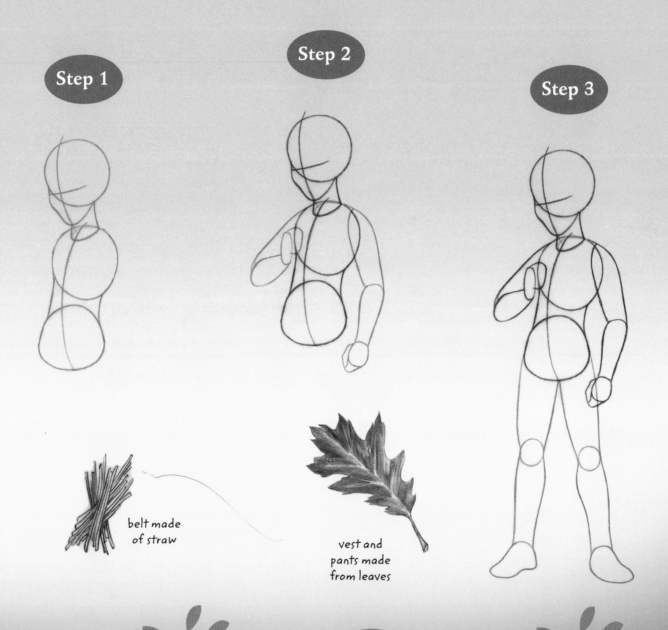

**Step 1**

**Step 2**

**Step 3**

belt made of straw

vest and pants made from leaves

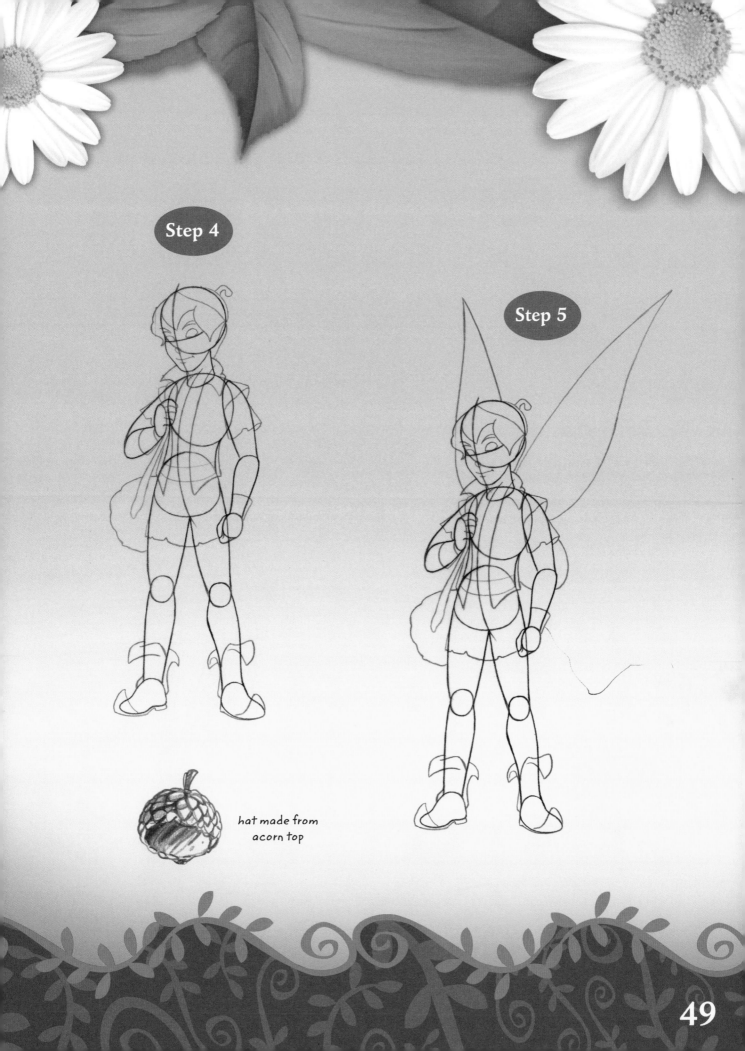

Step 4

Step 5

hat made from
acorn top

**Step 6**

**Step 7**

shoulder bag
made from
walnut shell

50

dispenses daily
rations of pixie dust

51

# Clank

Clank and Bobble are the very best of friends. There's no trouble these two tinkers haven't gotten into! They really admire Tinker Bell for her talent and skill.

**Step 1**

**Step 2**

**Step 3**

Clank puts cotton in his ears when he's working

carries a jug made from a nutshell

Clank is shaped like a fig

wears a
tunic made
of a leaf

Step 4

# Bobble

Bobble likes to hang out with his good friend Clank. These goofy pals love to fiddle, fix, craft, and create. Bobble's "glasses" are actually dewdrops set in blades of grass!

**Step 1**

**Step 2**

lens made of a dewdrop and a blade of grass

dewdrops make lenses look like bottle bottoms

Bobble's pants are made of moss

Bobble is
thin like
a twig

Step 3

Step 4

YES!
hair thick and
wavy on top;
short in back

NO!
hair not
flat and
long

# Chloe

Chloe teams up with Rosetta in the Pixie Hollow Games, despite the garden fairies' legendary losing streak. Chloe is an optimist and an idealist who is determined to break the streak for the garden fairies—and she's happy to get a little dirty along the way!

**Step 1**

**Step 2**

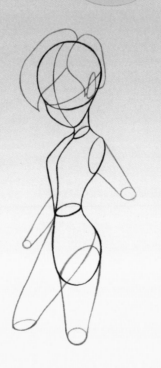

**Step 3**

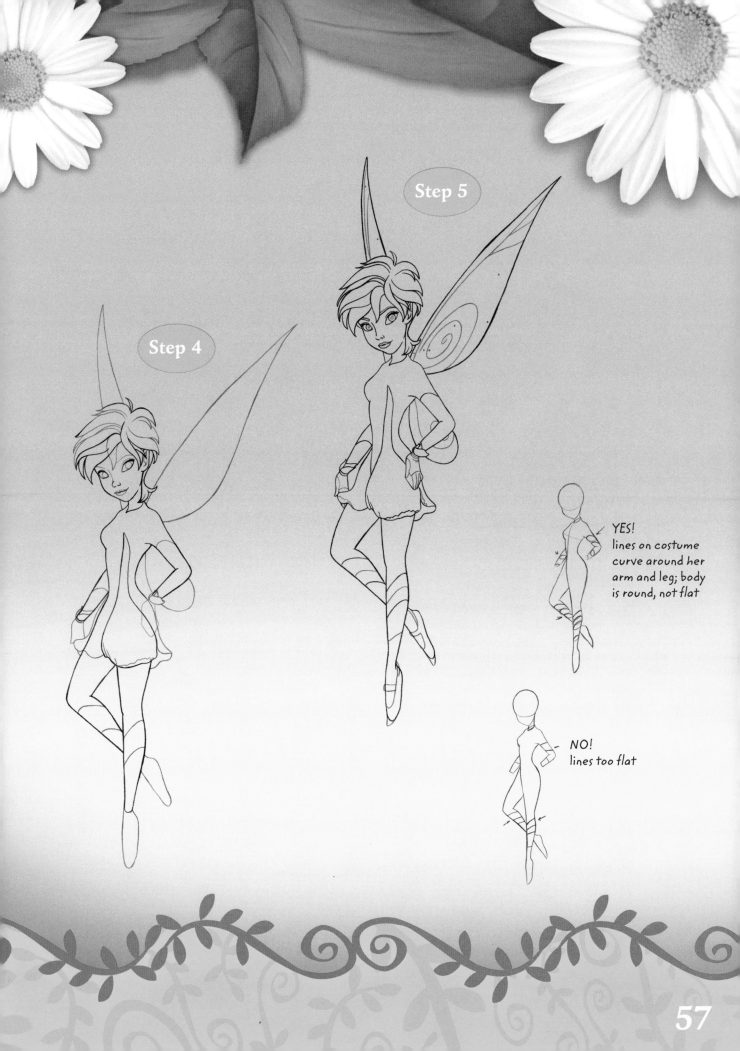

Step 5

Step 4

YES!
lines on costume
curve around her
arm and leg; body
is round, not flat

NO!
lines too flat

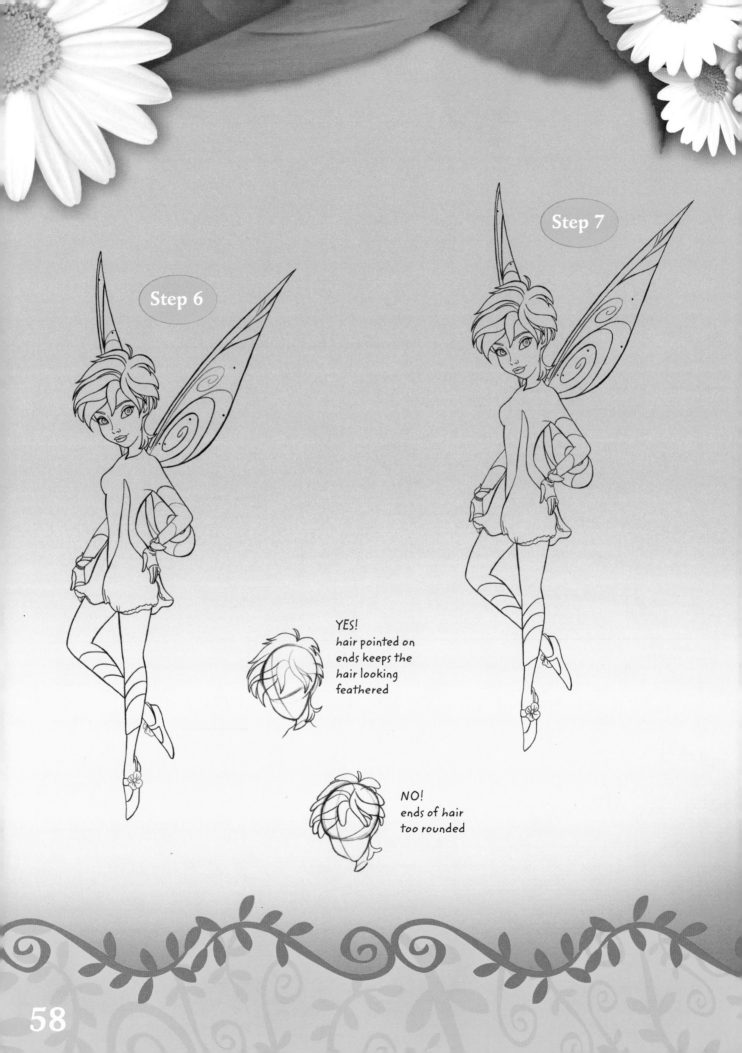

Step 6

Step 7

YES!
hair pointed on
ends keeps the
hair looking
feathered

NO!
ends of hair
too rounded

# Rumble

Rumble is a storm fairy who has won the Pixie Hollow Games with his partner, Glimmer, four years in a row! Rumble is cool, capable, and intimidating, and will stop at nothing in his attempts for a fifth ring.

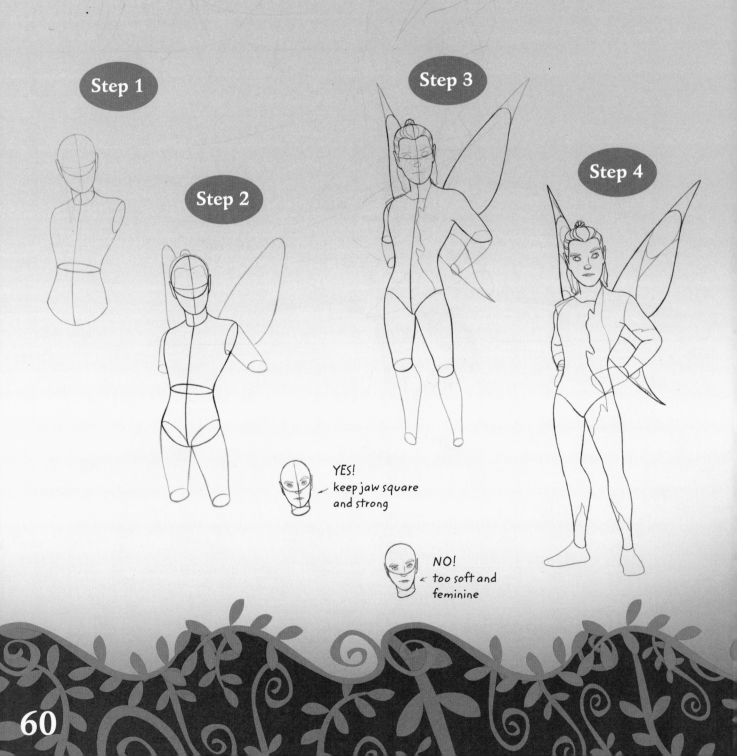

**Step 1**

**Step 2**

**Step 3**

**Step 4**

YES!
keep jaw square and strong

NO!
too soft and feminine

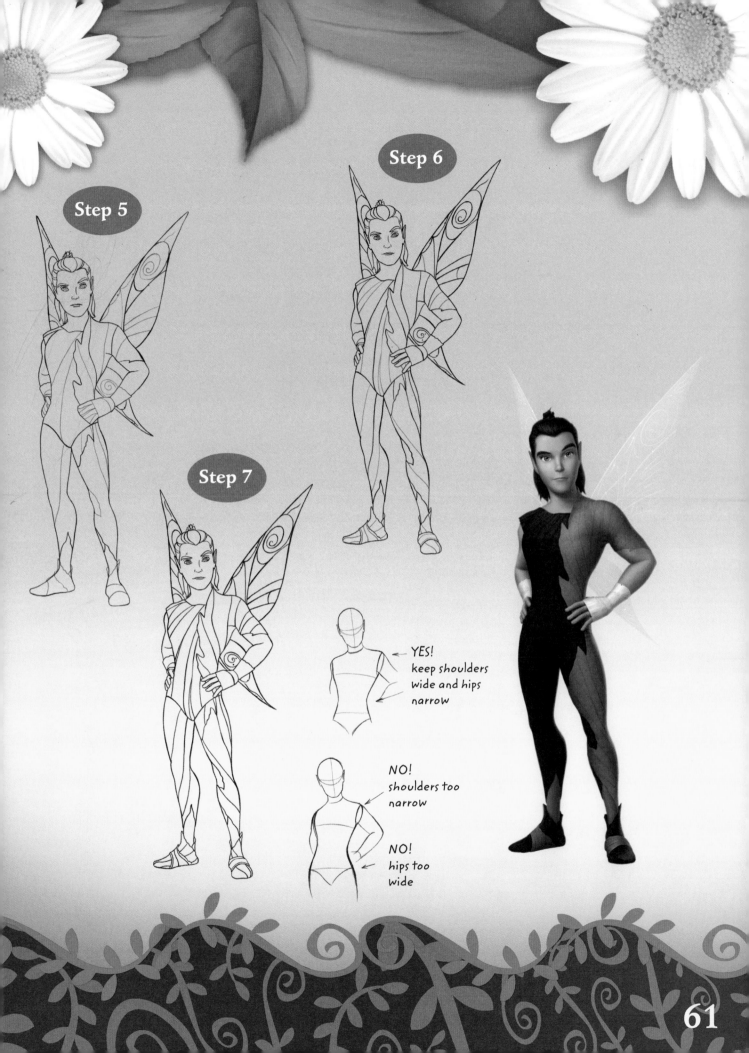

**Step 5**

**Step 6**

**Step 7**

→ YES!
keep shoulders
wide and hips
narrow

NO!
shoulders too
narrow

NO!
hips too
wide